DOROTHY PORTER

CRETE

*un*tapped

ABOUT *UNTAPPED*

Most Australian books ever written have fallen out of print and become unavailable for purchase or loan from libraries. This includes important local and national histories, biographies and memoirs, beloved children's titles, and even winners of glittering literary prizes such as the Miles Franklin Literary Award.

Supported by funding from state and territory libraries, philanthropists and the Australian Research Council, *Untapped* is identifying Australia's culturally important lost books, digitising them, and promoting them to new generations of readers. As well as providing access to lost books and a new source of revenue for their writers, the *Untapped* collaboration is supporting new research into the economic value of authors' reversion rights and book promotion by libraries, and the relationship between library lending and digital book sales. The results will feed into public policy discussions about how we can better support Australian authors, readers and culture.

See untapped.org.au for more information, including a full list of project partners and rediscovered books.

Readers are reminded that these books are products of their time. Some may contain language or reflect views that might now be found offensive or inappropriate.

for Andy

CONTENTS

Crete

Part 1

Crete 10

Linear A 11

The night before Knossos 13

Or else 14

My hairy sprog 15

Motherhood 17

Gorgeous breasts 18

Changed 19

Gross, green and mad 21

Grape dance 22

Rot here 23

A stinger! 24

The honey daimon 26

Part 2

Exuberance with bloody hands 28

Atlantis 30

Altars 32

Bull-leaping 34

Leaving Ariadne behind 35

Archaeology 36

The body 37

Lost civilisation 38

Uprooting trees 40

The Bride of Death 41

Wild honey 43

The Dead 44

What Death can do 46

The wine-dark sea 47
Blue monkey flying through an orchard 48
Snakes, stones and seeds 49
Snake envy 50
The flying leap 51
The law of volcanoes 53
The labyrinth of intimacy 54
Triumph of the Will 55
The Power and the Glory 56
Catastrophe 57
Vanished 58
Direst need 59
The beautiful friend 60
Liberties 61
Steering your seahorse 62

This Weird Solidarity
Telephone 64
Cherdyn 65
Moscow 68
Yelabuga 69

Missolonghi
· 1 · 72
· 2 · 73
· 3 · 74

Bone-burning Tunes
Why I Love Your Body 76
Mountains Window Edge 77
The Wailing Wall 79
For Beth In Gondwanaland 84
'The Stars Are Brightly Shining' 85
Stain 86
The Water 87
Hot Date 88
Music 91
The Emerald Leopard 92

Green Platypus Under A Toorak Palm 94
Starfish 95
Good Friday 97
The Flashing Mountain 98
Wives 100

Cigarettes

I 105
II 106
III 108
IV 109
V 110
VI 111
VII 112
VIII 114
IX 115
X 116
XI 117

Summer 92

As cunning as serpents 119
My at-last lover 120
Mud-crabs 121
Perfume and drowse 123
Lashed to the mast 124
Drought sonnet 126
'Stupid as a Poet' 127

Acknowledgements 136
Copyright 138

CRETE

'Blue island, give me back what is mine.
Flying Crete, give back my work to me.
Fill the baked vessel
from the breasts of the flowing goddess.'

Osip Mandelstam, 'Poem 385'

PART 1

The Trip

CRETE

Finding a vein
I find you

you're a wet socket
  of white sea

my tropical bikini top
  rips off

your blue eye
  won't lie flat
    on the broken wall

I twist like an otter
  in an underwater cave

your palaces are spiced
  with wine-dark
    chill

my chest echoes all night/all night
  on a thin mattress

your snake
  bites my breast
    with a hollow fang

O flash! O honey!

LINEAR A

When I was twenty-two
    just about everything was
        Linear A

I didn't understand
    that weird scribble
        in the belly
when I watched
    my prettier-than-me best friend
walking out of the green sea
    glimmering
        in her milky skin

I didn't understand
    Heraklion
its grit-grey port
    grotty even at sunrise
and its filthy youth hostel
I wanted
    to slide my thighs
        over the wet back
            of a blue dolphin
not squat and grunt
    over a shit-smeared hole

I didn't understand
    that photos
    of my own young
        exuberantly tanned face

would sink
    and one day wave
like frantic tentacles
    from an octopus pot.

THE NIGHT BEFORE KNOSSOS

On the deck
   of a Crete-bound ferry
two young women
   sleep badly
      under a green raincoat

the engine room
   thumps
      through their ribs

stars, diesel, spray
   coat them
      in a glistening salt.

OR ELSE

No sensible woman eats poppies

   or else

she'll dance
she'll fall over

she'll wake up

     with a woman in her arms.

MY HAIRY SPROG

In myths
    I always go for
        the tart, the witch
            the feral girl.

Wasn't Pasiphaë
        smart
to find a way
        to fuck
            her spunky white bull?

Who says
    Poseidon made her do it?

Skewered
    on that beast's
        steaming pizzle
she probably got more
    than she bargained for

but she lived
    to boast about it

and spawn
    her own hairy sprog

who's still howling
    through the marvellous
        palace plumbing.

Is he
　　why I'm nervous
　　　　of the unnatural consequences
　　　　　　of my unnatural acts?

MOTHERHOOD

No longer will she
    flash
       like *Fantasia*
          across the sea floor

the giant octopus is dying

in her blue den
    her clusters of eggs
       swell like cysts

the giant octopus is dying

her moody vivid nervous system
    shut down and dun

the giant octopus is dying

her tentacles wave
like drowned arms
    her ink bubbles away

the giant octopus is dying

she's got nothing left
her eggs took the lot.

GORGEOUS BREASTS

After our first time
    we went to a Chinese restaurant
    and counted on our
        charged fingers

the relatives
the friends
    who'd never be the same

we were breathless
in the high wind
of our secret

that first kiss
like a dancer
    in the bullring
flying
    over the bull's horns
        on a quick breath

what a flirt
before the gorgeous breasts
    of the crowd!

CHANGED

'...changed, changed utterly:
A terrible beauty is born.'
                    W. B. Yeats

I'll never change

never never

no utterly about it

it's you

   you've changed

      utterly utterly

have you always been

   terribly beautiful?

change

     my hands are spilling silver

   I'm dumbfounded

I've changed

   utterly terrible

20

as I born this way?

you touch me

    utterly utterly

      beautiful

no terrible about this

I wasn't born into it

you've chosen me.

GROSS, GREEN AND MAD

My garden
is not a labyrinth

I'd like to make it
more mysterious
and less work

if I ignore it
the blackberry takes over

if I ignore it
the pot plants die

if I ignore it
it goes gross, green
and mad

if I ignore it
it will attack the house
like an allergy

if I ignore it
it won't go quietly

if I ignore it
it won't be a labyrinth

it will be the Minotaur.

GRAPE DANCE

The air
    empty
        and full

the moment
    grapes

our mouths
    purple

our feet
    tangle
        and drop

sipping this
    sweet dance

all of me
all of you

ROT HERE

In the dark
I'm a miracle

in the dark
I'm a coffin

in the dark
I'm taking off my shirt

breasts!

the earth bubbling
under a rose bush

in the dark
my hair grows stealthily

in the dark
I confess

I don't wanna go to heaven
I wanna rot here.

A STINGER!

I tell the withered
    teenage mothers
        on cold railway stations

I tell the packed animals
    fighting for their footing
        on the slope
            to the abattoir

when will I tell myself?

my throat is cut

but I'm still standing!

my blood is honey
my words are bees

my heart
    is a stinger!

I tell the queues
    in public hospitals
        swaying on swollen hips

how easy to believe
    we are living in Hell

but

my throat is cut

and I'm still standing!

our blood is honey
our words are bees

our heart
   is a stinger!

THE HONEY DAIMON

'Life is for the daimons and the demons,
those that put honey on our lips, and those that put salt.'
            D. H. Lawrence

This morning
    is whiter than salt

a daimon of blossom!

gorgeous, dishabille

touching me up
    in an ear-aching wind

don't flirt with me, Spring

thaw
    and I'm in big trouble

I run
    like honey

and drool
    in anybody's mouth.

PART 2

There

'take care, do not know me,
deny me, do not recognise me,

shun me; for this reality
is infectious – ecstasy.'

H. D.

EXUBERANCE WITH BLOODY HANDS

What do the Minoans teach us—
exuberance with bloody hands?

The wind the Goddess brings
is both wonderful and vicious

she flies into your soul
she flies into your face

and what will you do to see her?

Become the stone altar
become the moist fetish
become the bird screaming down on you

it's just a trance
you tell yourself
you'll wake up tomorrow
your lover sleeping on your shoulder

it was just the wine
it was just the drugs

it's all over
I can't remember
nothing happened

no-one got hurt

but there was something
a wind, a bird, a sense
of being taken up and over

dancing and dying
dancing and not dying
dancing and living forever

but your mortal lover snores
and snuffles into your mortal skin

the rattle, the trees, that perfume,
that fantastic presence

what are you fit for now?

whose throat would you cut
to have it happen again?

ATLANTIS

'...but when the divine portion began to fade slowly, and became diluted too often and too much with the mortal admixture, and the human nature got the upper hand, they then, being unable to bear their fortune, behaved unseemly, and to him who had an eye to see grew visibly debased, for they were losing the fairest of their precious gifts; but to those who had no eye to see the true happiness, they appeared glorious and blessed at the very time they were becoming tainted with unrighteous ambition and power.'

From Plato's account of Atlantis in Critias

'Each time a victim was beaten to death they started to clap.'
Eyewitness account of pogroms in Lithuania, 1941

Were there Lithuanians in Atlantis?

Or was it all glorious
among the slithering lilies?

Under the abscessed tooth of history
we believe in a clean golden socket
we call Atlantis

where fountains, voices, frescoes
and fabulous cities
all refract

into memory-aching rainbows
arching under the ocean.

Where did it go?
how could we have lost it?

How convenient to ignore
the smell, the mouldy smell
of human rising damp

like tenants in a cheap house
we learn to live, eat and sleep
in it

while the water table laps
our foundations
with a rotting tongue.

Do we really want to know
we never got it right?

Atlantis threw the young
of its captive cities
to the horns of the bulls

in the festive smell of blood
the crowd clapped

and primped
before the envy of the future.

ALTARS

Is the gaily painted trussed bull
still alive
as its slashed neck bleeds
into the sacred vessel?

Every altar in Crete
must have reeked
of the fluids of terror—
diarrhoea and fresh blood.

Why do the stainless steel altars
in our laboratories
smell sweeter?

What do we learn
from the dog
lying red-raw
at the Burn Institute?

Ask the cat
fixed still
in a stereotaxic device
for a fiddling PhD.

These modern clever fingers
that flick the switch

these modern clever fingers
that click up the results

don't need to scrub themselves
clean
like the public priests
of Potnia and Poseidon—

there is no disinfectant
as effective as cold reason.

We may have inherited deafness
from Crete

but the room-freshener
is all our own.

BULL-LEAPING

Is poetry a strange leftover
of Minoan bull-leaping?

the archaic skill
of flying over the back
of the beast

and gracefully surviving,
making it look easy

the bare sweaty breasts
the gilded loin cloth

the crowd enjoying
your big sexy risk.

Or is this kind of poetry
a forgotten fresco crumbling
under a mound of prose

the pieces glimmering
like snakes scuttling to ground?

LEAVING ARIADNE BEHIND

Why point the finger at Theseus?
Haven't we all done it?

It may not have been
as brutal as choice.

You bury the clay charm
in your garden

you're numb

you pray to do
the right thing

then the wind comes up
with an urgent freshness

the breath of your fate

you move to the ship
your hands set the sail

don't think
fate tells you

don't say goodbye.

ARCHAEOLOGY

Am I the Arthur Evans
of my own lost city?

Excavated
with shovelling obsession

Restored
with wishful thinking?

Glint. Glint. Glint.

The sun picks over my trash
for treasure.

And on my layers
of gleaming silt

Stamp the thick legs
of a cement palace.

THE BODY

Is the changing body ever
as glorious as the changing tree?

Can the body flow into autumn
as rapturously?

A cheetah lolls in the grass,
all gaze, all coiled grace.

My eye springs on its image
carnivorously.

If I eat the cheetah
will I be the cheetah?

The greying Minoan lifts
his boar-faced knife

over the altar
over the lovely boy

if I eat the boy
will I be the boy?

LOST CIVILISATION

*'Throughout the killing in the Colosseum a band would
play...'*

BBC Documentary

How did the stories of mythology become
mass-spectacle pom?

For the woman prisoner playing Pasiphaë
for the bull tormented into mounting her
there was no sociological puzzle

just this moment

the woman's ripping uterus
the bull's heaving fear

the terrible smell
of each other

the stinging hornet music.

Did the spiced imagination
of the Minoans
arouse the carrion palate
of the Romans

to give the world
its first performance
of snuff theatre?

UPROOTING TREES

Is my blood too thin
to serve the gods of ecstasy?

Where is the wind
that plucked out the wall-flower
and flung her
into the jiving embrace
of the homed stag?

Something's not right with me.
I wander heavy in my body.
Three parts chlorinated water
one part cask wine.

Take me to the Minoan party.
Watch the Goddess shimmy-shimmy
watch her fancy man
            uprooting trees.

THE BRIDE OF DEATH

'I have left weaving at the loom for greater things,
For hunting beasts with my bare hands.'

Euripides, The Bacchae

Who is waiting for me
at the heart of the Labyrinth?

How will he smell my coming?

I haven't yet woven the scent
of my wedding gown

the scent of ready meat.

Why has my Lady given me away
prematurely?

No soap will ever slip
the scorching ring off my finger.

She refused me postponement
or thread.

My eyes are wide
stuck open with dread.

The invisible drip
the only music

down this invisible aisle.

Should I grow claws
should I lick my lips

and hunt him instead?

O, my lord, you are very lovely.

Who is the bull?
Who is the cow?

Open wide
   this won't hurt a bit.

WILD HONEY

Can the insects suckle us?

A swarm of bees fed infant Zeus
in a Cretan mountain cave
honey not milk.

Imagine your nursing mother
with wings, a sting
and a buzz.

Would your skin crawl?

We are born with a tooth
sweet to know the alien

sweet
to know the winged buzzing ones
stings and all.

When does our skin learn to crawl?

When do we learn revenge?
And how to pour petrol
    over the hive
        of our terrifying mothers.

THE DEAD

'Though of weak faith, I believe in forces and powers
Who crowd every inch of the air.
They observe us — is it possible that no one sees us?'

Czeslaw Milosz

How did the Minoans cross the line
between the quick and the dead?

did they dance over it?

their ghosts waiting
in ecstatic mid-air?

We have found the top quark
but lost our dead.

Are our most violent poltergeists
books?

gnashing their shelves
smashing things in the dark

they leave a greenish tombish
smell on our reading fingers

they make us musty
and bereft.

The Minoans didn't read
their ghosts

they sniffed
their blue perfume

and went wild on them.

WHAT DEATH CAN DO

'No more let Life divide what Death can join together.'

P. B. Shelley, 'Adonais'

What did Death do for the Minoans?

Did Death flash among them
    like distraught lightning?

Winter is no sleep
    when grief keeps you
        on your burning toes

you dance the god's bones
to glass

you dance the god's bones
    to a mirror

Who is it?

that long hair
    dripping
        like a stalactite
            into your eyes?

You dance blind
    for a dead face
        being born again

you dance for yourself.

THE WINE-DARK SEA

Did the Minoans discover
how to drink the sea?

Or did the malice of salt water
send Crete mad?

The sea grows wonderful
   glittering
      and huge
like a monster grape

it is not
   the warm belly
where we stay forever
   the lulled and loved foetus

it is the most fertile
   of temptations

exhilarating poison
   spawning in us
      a gasping art

a futile sensuality.

BLUE MONKEY FLYING THROUGH AN ORCHARD

After Arthur Boyd's painting
* 'Swan flying through an orchard'*

Why are Minoan paintings
    so mischievously lovely?

Their landscapes
    like nothing on earth

but wafty with sticky smell
    like a thrumming orchard.

And something wondrous strange
    flying through the triffid-waving
        branches

a blue monkey
    lighter than life

gibbering
    I'm here   I'm here

SNAKES, STONES AND SEEDS

When will the Lady thrust her breasts
in my face again?

When will my listless snakes
suck her milk?

I have lost half my seeds.

My lost ovary shrivelling
on some male pathologist's
steel dish.

What have they cut out of me?

Seeds. But not snakes.
Not stones.

For now let me lie
fallow
    in my hissing rubble.

SNAKE ENVY

When did we lose the knack
   of handling snakes
      with exquisite familiarity?

Snakes bluish
   with leopard spots
boil over the breasts, arms
      and throat
      of the Minoan priestess

she gazes through
   our uneven breathing

we're nothing to her

our fear has a nasty smell

we want the snakes
   to bite her.

THE FLYING LEAP

*'Sometimes we detect a grim humour, as where a
Minotaur appears to be devouring his own hand...'*

Arthur Evans on the Zakro seals,
The Palace of Minos at Knossos

Why did Ikaros's flying leap
take him too close to the sun?

Perhaps
      rather than reckless
            he was shivering

he was mouldy cold.

You can take the boy
out of the labyrinth

you can't take the labyrinth
out of the boy

he could smell the Minotaur
            playing in his own mind

he could feel the Minotaur
      growing horns
            through his own skin.

Only the sun

could melt this tumour

only the sun
        could stump
            the devouring maze.

THE LAW OF VOLCANOES

'Every peak is a crater. This is the law of volcanoes'

Adrienne Rich

What made the Minoans
so volatilely feminine?

What honey narcotic seethed
from the roaring crack
under their toenails?

Did their strange flirt
with this dangerous world
go straight to their pretty heads?

And now
    they're a wafting tease

they promise you paradise.

Smell them hovering

        hot feathers, old ash.

  Play hard to get.

THE LABYRINTH OF INTIMACY

*'Beyond the strength of any other act of witness, literature
and the arts tell of the obstinacies of the impenetrable, of
the absolutely alien which we come up against in the lab-
yrinth of intimacy. They tell of the Minotaur at the heart
of love, of kinship, of utmost confiding.'*

George Steiner

How far did the Minoan thread go
in the labyrinth of intimacy?

Was there less tear and tangle
when they loved their dead
more than each other?

The world of gorgeous hallucination
is a sweeter place to visit
than the mucky lair of another's heart.

The Minotaur helpless
   the Minotaur bleating blind
      in the brutal sun

is this the truth of love
none of us could bear?

TRIUMPH OF THE WILL

Were the Minoans brutal
in their rapture
for athletic glory?

Were they just podgy perving Nazis
hooked on an endless beefcake movie
of poncing curls, impossible waists
and lingering shots of loincloths?

The beautiful boy, the beautiful girl,
    perfect and provocative
        in their fragrant bravery

let's stick them in the ring.

We'll starve
        and flatter them
we'll shift our arses
        on our seats
and watch the beasts
        platter them.

THE POWER AND THE GLORY

'...not one single example has been brought to light of any subject of an indecorous nature.'

Arthur Evans

Was sex too sacred
for the Minoans to leave behind
    or too insignificant?

In what other time
has the breast been mightier
    than the sword?

CATASTROPHE

Do you ever live long enough?

The crisp morning, your step brisk
walking into its current

humming breath, happy belly,
a skinful of pleasure.

But like Crete
this morning won't last

your isle of lilies will blow up
in a stinking roar

your calm sea will curdle
into catastrophe

and the tapeworm of horror
will hatch its eggs.

There'll be nothing
but morphine, black humour

and prayers for a shovel
from a kind and curious future

to guess what you were
and dig you back.

VANISHED

It's the little things
    that vanish
it's the little things
    we grieve for.

Was the Prince of Lilies
    leading a royal griffin
        or showing off his dog?

The fresco fragments give us
    his left hand clutching
        a snapped-off lead

only his amazing head-dress intact.

An extravagant boy
    deified by extravagant art
    deaf to personal questions.

Why am I living
    cloistered in his mystery?

Why won't his right fist
    clenched over his crumbling chest
unclench
        over my breathing breast?

DIREST NEED

*'The little gold and ivory image, restored once more to the light
of day, is that of a Goddess, always still a Mother, but who,
it may be in some more celestial scene, herself had shared the
most risky turns of the sport. We have here, in fact, a record of
some such glittering vision as had comforted of old the strained
eyes of her followers in the moment of their direst need.'*

Arthur Evans

Some moments have the clarity
of your own exposed
        teeth and bones

you lie
        broken and wide-awake
                under the bull's breath

you can call her name
you can whimper for
        the billow of her breasts

your world slits
        to a pause

you're waiting

for a glory of ivory
        and gold
                to leap in and save you.

THE BEAUTIFUL FRIEND

The Minoans moulded the crust
   of the sea
      on to their pottery

as if their beautiful friend
   would one day
      dry up.

Drink from us, Lady,
their barnacled cups urge

feel us, feel the rough
of our shells in your hand

let us fill you up.

Nothing is more passionate
   than a Minoan octopus

whirling from the artist's heart
with eight arms
to clutch the receding tide.

What can our numb fingers make
   to console
      our beautiful friend?

LIBERTIES

'The secret of life is Art'

Oscar Wilde

The Minoans took greater liberties
   with nature
than squinting Arthur ever took
   with them

   blue birds, flowering ivy,
     wild roses with an impossible
       number of petals

a reckless geyser
   blooming over polished agate

they painted what they fancied
   not what they saw.

STEERING YOUR SEAHORSE

'The golden Muses gave me
true riches: when dead
I shall not be forgotten.'

Sappho

Perhaps the Minoans only sacrificed
boys.

I can't see that busty priestess
steering her seahorse
through the bucking water
handing over her daughter.

Unless she dedicated her girl
to the bulls
fastened a necklace around
her frightened throat
gave her balls in a pretty
codpiece

show them, darling,
she whispered

be brave.
steer your seahorse.

THIS WEIRD SOLIDARITY

All quotes are from *nightingale fever—Russian Poets in Revolution* by Ronald Hingley (Alfred A. Knopf, New York, 1981)

TELEPHONE

'While Mandelstam languished under interrogation in the Lubyanka's dungeons in central Moscow [1934], Akhmatova and Pasternak were trying to rescue him by appealing to influential colleagues of Stalin... Mandelstam's fate still hung in the balance when Stalin suddenly made it the subject for an unheralded telephone call to Pasternak.'

The Colossus pulled my leash.
Am I a leopard?
Or am I its feast?

A casual chat about Poetry.
Is this the live wire
to lead us from the cemetery?

At last my curtain call.
Will this big cat Hamlet
take a pratfall?

I swished up to Mister History.
'Life and Death', I threw him
the boldest bait of mystery.

But, Osip, forgive me,
History slammed down the phone.

CHERDYN

'Consignment to Cherdyn was the nearest thing possible to being sent to Siberia while still remaining within European Russia... Mandelstam was still showing symptoms of mental disorder... His obsessive delusions included the notion that Anna Akhmatova had recently been executed somewhere in the area; he scoured nearby gullies for her corpse.' [1934]

Five nights, Anna

I can hear your elegant voice

counting them out
    like smoke rings

Five nights, Anna

I couldn't sleep

if I closed one eye
or – horror – if
    I closed two

that axe

    would fall

I haven't slept
    for five days, Anna

my wife say
 'Sleep, Osip,
   sleep now
find Anna
  after you have slept'

they've murdered you

sleep can come
sleep can fold me up
   and put me in a drawer

when I have found you

I'll put you back together, Anna
  like a poem

I'll bite you
  out of my frozen thumbs

and make you

Anna! our Trojan Horse!

can we keep Boris
    from chattering

or Marina
  from banging her
    spear on your wall?

'Shut up, Boris'

'Keep still, Marina'

how much breeze in your whisper!

I'm not love-sick, Anna

kisses! kisses! like frozen bulbs

can I kiss your dead face?

no winter
   can stop us
      pushing through
         our amazing heads.

MOSCOW

*'It is astonishing that Russia's two most celebrated women
poets... should never have come face to face before [early
1940]. And it is regrettable that we know so little of what
passed between them. Akhmatova has said that Tsveta-
yeva spoke brilliantly...'*

We were sitting in a park
stripped to its bones.

For the first time in months
I forgot my old stove

and bin of green potatoes.

Marina, you were a packet
of American cigarettes

I smoked you to the filter.

Where were we?

Under bare trees
in a park stripped to its bones.

YELABUGA

'...she retired to Yelabuga utterly weary and desperate... de-
clining the only employment offered to her, as dishwasher
in a canteen. On Sunday 31 August [1941] Marina Ivanov-
na [Tsvetayeva] hanged herself from a hook... The towns-
people had never heard of her or her poetry, and no-one,
not even her son, attended her burial in the local cemetery.'

I had a lot of fun
    loving badly

my infatuations
    were glossy rats

who followed my pipe
    merrily enough

so what
    I couldn't kiss Osip's eyelashes
      forever

or drag out my Prague lover's
    tears

or speed up Anna
    with my comet hands

or crackle Boris
    with my crossed wires

so—
    who's complaining?

It's just because
    I'm running out of cigarettes

that I'm whimpering

another dare

another empty swimming pool

jump!
    hit the water
    with your legs straight

but I've spent
    my whole life
    making belly-flops!

you're old, Marina

the rats
    are no longer enchanted

snap goes the weasel
crack goes my throat.

MISSOLONGHI

"Tis time this heart should be unmoved.'

Byron, Jan. 22 1824, Greece

· I ·

Even the leeches, Loukas,
        don't bleed
my lust for astonishment

how does the heart
    that disobedient pump
        make its choice?

why do I drag
    myself out of bed

every morning

just to watch you?

· 2 ·

I'm not really asleep, Loukas

I'm only foxing
　　so I can watch you
　　　　moving about my room

take it, take it,
　　it's only my watch
　　　　I've had a gutful of Time

hold its old gold finish
　　against your smooth cheek

tick. tick. tick. tick.
　　like an old heart

how can I roar out of bed
　　and blame you
　　　　for stealing from me?

I've sacked and looted
　　everyone I've ever loved.

· **3** ·

Last night I dreamt
I took you pistol shooting

it was a ghost dawn
the ground was smoking

but your face was clear

I have dreamt
stars like tar pits
I have dreamt
an arrow sticking out
of a defeated eye

last night, Loukas,
I dreamt

we were pistol shooting

the ground was smoking
a ghost dawn.

BONE-BURNING TUNES

WHY I LOVE YOUR BODY

I put your body
   between me
      and the history of horrors

your sweet tongue
snaking through my lips

your heavy breasts
thudding ripe on my ribs

your thin legs climbing mine
like twin grape vines

your creamy wetness
creeping through my fingers

when your body bursts over me
my mind goes almost quiet
faintly squeaking to itself
like a fruit bat dozing
      upside down.

I put your body
   between me
      and the terrifying future
         of my body

tonight I'm a noisy swamp
squelching under your bare toes.

MOUNTAINS WINDOW EDGE

for Judy Beveridge

Is it mescaline
   on the quiet
      but constant boil
somewhere
   in the tight wet battery
      of my cortex?

Is it some fey gen
   from blue-eyed Fay
my grandmother
   who would perk up
      in the back seat of a car
   to love the colour
      of the sea
as we rose over the hill
   to Mona Vale?

In the centre
   of my tooth-grinding
      eye-squint of a self
is an eye-still
      wonder

that never hurries
through the light-tousled
body of the Goddess

who looks at the red breast
of a parrot
in a bare but budding tree

as if my own bright blood
    was untraumatically
        on show

life, life, life

the white trunk
of a young gum
    in the cold dusk

the amethyst of wine
    drunk too fast
        to Ella Fitzgerald
as the window fogs
        in my looking-out breath

to stay with the light
    picking out
        the last of the plum blossoms

is to go luxuriant dusk
    myself

the fade of my veins
the glimmer of my hands

a slow intoxicated dissolve
    from red to blue.

THE WAILING WALL

The skin on my hand
   last night
glowed olive-dark
   from the cuff
      of a white silk shirt

distracting me

I watched it
   with a slow narcissism

I watched it
   holding a drink
I watched it
   still and mysterious
      on my heavy leg

and once again
   I couldn't talk
      to my dead grandmother

even to say
   thank you
for my gypsy hand
   that is bloody useless
but good to look at
under a soft lamp

good
    for waving prettily
        in the air

thank you, Gran
I'm sober now

thank you
    for giving me
        your skin

my skin

you were darker
    darker
        than me

what did you call it
    in others?

this darkness
this skin that glows
    under a light

black blood, black blood

who were you
    prickling in your skin?

what did you do
    with your small dark hands
        that could sew, cook, crochet
           and prune a rose

that never talked
   like some jabbering foreigner
      in the air

that bunched in gloves
   drove a car,
      when women didn't drive,
that bunched in fists
   sat like stones
      on your lap

they were useful hands, Gran

they worked for you
   like sullen slaves

on their own time
   they had other business

old, old business

they were stiff-necked hands
it didn't matter
   that you denied them
      their temple, their people
         their strange
            and domineering place in the world

they knew their birthright
they knew what to do to you

didn't you ever notice
   the veils over your mirrors?

didn't you ever notice
   the discreet tear
      in your perfect clothes?

they were at work
   your hands, your hands
      were sitting shiva over you

Hyman, Cohen, Aarons, Meyer
   and Brodziak

Nathan, Saartje, Aloe, de Leeuw
   and Leefson

your fingers had circumcised names
   your hands muttered them
      like curses

so what did you curse
   while they cursed you?

you cursed your skin
your dark skin   your dark skin

you cursed it
   wherever you saw it

you cursed it
   in Africa

you cursed it
   in a migrant face

you cursed it
   in your grand-daughter

with her useless hands
   that glowed at night
      like your hands

     your busy hands.

FOR BETH IN GONDWANALAND

A king parrot
in a bare tree
moulting drifts of snow—

Gondwanaland shifts south
and the silence arrives—

a stranger crunches
through my white garden
trespassing with deep black marks—

Beth
who has just died
talks to me
affectionately
in my head.

'THE STARS ARE BRIGHTLY SHINING'

After aria from Tosca

What do we bury
in ourselves?

What do we bury
at nightfall?

Those grinning glittering faces
those piercing bits and pieces
that move us
to pace the house
change the record—

the spilled intestines
of memory
caught in our hands

catching us out
in astonished anguish.

STAIN

If you must mark me
make it pretty

give me a birthmark
the colour of an orchid
so inviting
my lover will sniff it
like a blissed bee

embroider my wrist
with a tattoo
so my talking hand
can trail in the air
a glimpse of the exquisite

if you must keep me
in this skin

if you will never let me out

don't make me live inside
stained walls

make them pretty.

THE WATER

It's the water I remember,
the warm salt-lick silk of it
around my half-grown hand

and the air
crackling with hot holiday smells,
sausages, eucalyptus and Aerogard

was it one moment
on that rocking pontoon
or a thousand?

was it one time
I chanted to myself
remember, remember, remember?

the water. my hand. summer.
my life cooking up a storm.

and my loneliness
electric.

HOT DATE

Pine trees
   come most alive
      dripping with resin
        in a fire

I've got a hot date
   with Death

will she be
   my boiling Celt?

will we dare
   the White Horses?

dewy together
   Death and I

hot-sea blue

or will Death
   be my curly corkscrew
      Jew?

'I'm you
I'm you'
she moans

knocking me to the floor
of an old blood hotel
sucking out my breath

Oh Death!

I never knew you
  in a dress
  in high heels

just the melt
  of your breasts
the forklift
  of your tongue

I can't bring home
  a devil
    to meet my mother

but I won't
  ring for a taxi

I'm not leaving

until you tell me
  about yourself

  let's talk, Death

can't we be friends?

is it all
        sex
      with you?

do you like cricket?
do you like tennis?

what did you think
 of this year's Film Festival?

Sip your long black
 slowly, Death

I want to know you

do you want
 to be my second cousin
  twice-removed?

Celt or Jew.

You'll never be English, Death

I said Goodbye To All That
 with my last Anglican
  Communion

I can't remember
 the wafer
I couldn't get drunk
 on the wine

Celt or Jew.

Breath or dew.

You'll never be faithful.
I'll never be true.

Because, Death,
 I'm not simple

and neither are you.

MUSIC

for Andy

'my soul in my precious lyre
will survive my ashes and avoid decay'

Pushkin

My decaying lyre
   glows green
under the rubbish mounds

dumped
it lies in wait
for someone's fossicking fingers

what bone-burning tunes
it will play
through that stray hand!

THE EMERALD LEOPARD

You're lost if you steer.

How did you get here?

Leopard, that smell in the air.
Leopard, that spoor at your feet.

Your knots unfurled into a sail
and you tacked into a high colour

green.

The leopard coughs from the horizon
you head for her throat.

She's beautiful.

A roar of sea, a roar of fur
you can look at her
you can look at anything.

A whiplash of tail
as she looks at you.

She's so dangerous;
immense,
she takes your trembling measure

her eyes smoke

your eyes close

you want the cuff of her paw
you dream
of her weight on your chest.

She doesn't move.
A lush silence
spreads from her stare.

Her breath in your face.

She shapes you
sharp as light.

You don't swoon.

GREEN PLATYPUS UNDER A TOORAK PALM

After Frank O'Hara

This Melbourne winter
        I'm sunbaking
a green platypus under a Toorak palm dumb monotreme
lonely and happy off/on laying the odd leathery egg
how much time
        does it take to know a new city a new
heart running sideways like a crab?
while on the tram Fellini meets the United Nations
    the drivers are bizarre
        I'm too bored to be a racist, the stranger the
better, bring on the freaks, bring on the accent and
    the garlic and that green monsoon of hotel upside
        down   and full of possibility
let me not stay sad nostalgic and silly and
        talking to the dusk spooks
        there's enough shivers in Melbourne so let me
thrill
        to a tropic in my own head
            my deluxe river bank where Mrs Platypus
                that chic little duckbill comes home with
                    the bacon turns off my sunlamp
and is just beside herself
                to have me living here

STARFISH

Goebbels was right.

You can be told
    to hate anything.

Yesterday
    the starfish
        so many, so white,
        so close to the dock
in the green light
            off Hobart
sent me rapt
    like Coleridge's old mariner
        taking coils of sea snake
            to his bosom.

Today
    the Museum told me
the starfish
    are foreigners
    are breeding like rats
    are gobbling them
        who belong here.

They're going to round you up, starfish,
    and get rid of you—

no escape
no descendants

with a scatter of your genes
to mourn
and try and breed
you back

there'll be clear water
and just the usual
rubbish.

GOOD FRIDAY

The road outside
is waiting for me

waiting for me
to do things differently

prepare yourself, it's saying
prepare yourself for praying

The road outside
is empty and inglorious

I clench my black spanner
and dream murder instead

The road outside
is waiting for me

prepare yourself, it's saying,
for the emptiness of praying

and the shadow of Earth
passing over your dying moon.

THE FLASHING MOUNTAIN

I have come to the end
   of so many old things

I have come to the end
   of the world

to wait for this mountain
   to flash

flash like a cloud
   struggling with light

flash like a tense second
   of white steel

I'm slack enough
   to hear

the low orange music
   of a foraging cat

I'm slack enough
   to follow

a sea-eagle
   arrogant with sky

I have come to the end
   of so many things

I have come to the end
   of my world

to wait for this mountain
   to flash.

WIVES

There's a darkness in women's warmth
there's a trapdoor in women's talk

I married for warmth
I married for talk

forever, we said
exchanging vows over cigarettes and cappuccinos

forever, we said
toasting ourselves in an empty house

And who did we marry?

I married the moon
I married my silver remotest self

she married the mirror
she married an echo of ravishing kisses

lightning strikes/melting skin
we lived in an electrical storm

we didn't care who paid the bills
we didn't care who swept the floor

we had the moon, we had the mirror
we smelted silver in echoing kisses

forever, we said
holding hands on the street

forever, we said
giving up our friends

each other's fantastic familiar
like flying black cats

each other's eyes and ears
like spies in a black-wise thriller

we muffled our clocks
we blurred our faces

we tick. tick. ticked. like silky bombs
under each other's breasts

day and night ran together
like whirling dyes in a wild wash

And what was the world
without our joined pulse?

it trashed and trafficked
monotonously beyond our walls

she was wine
I was delicious insomnia

awake and intoxicated
we talked up shimmering lives

where we were the crackling streets
where we were the diamond constellations

fire and smoke gusted us about
we floated in the air like torched cities

forever, we said
over New Year valley sunsets

forever, we said
wearing each other's caressing clothes

the lawn grew to our necks
the vacuum cleaner choked

our house closed its threadbare fist
around our dancing ankles

we tripped
we fell on each other

it's her fault
it's her fault

our echoing thoughts resentful
our echoing thoughts finding each other

you're not me
you're not me

in bed there's always present tense
zipped in each other we ignore the phone

It was the world calling

girls, it called through the dustmotes
girls, it called through our mouths

I unmarry you
I unmarry you

we're wives, we replied
our hair tangled like blackberry vines

we're wives, we screamed
tearing roots and scalp

we're free, we groaned
touching the air where our other had breathed.

CIGARETTES

I

The dove of peace
   no longer brings
      an olive branch

the dove of peace
   offers the halo
      of the shared cigarette

that glow
   between your lover's fingers
is the red-tipped palm
   on your oasis

it smoke-signals
   your shared
      alert drowse

you have never heard
   the war so hushed.

I I

My grandfather's
   silver cigarette case
has a battered elegance;
his civilised friend
   who'd slip so smoothly
      into a pocket
over my grandfather's
      heart
when the shelling started
      up again
in the trenches of Amiens,
now sits
   stained but cool
      in my hand—

I don't remember
   my grandfather
      smoking
or talking about
   the War—

I remember
   his light step
   his cartoon portrait gallery
      of his grandchildren
         painted
      around the cracks
         of the garage wall—

and the heart attack
    that burst from nowhere
      and killed him.

III

Relief
   brings out cigarettes
like the passing of a storm
   brings out the happiness
      of frogs

I know
   you always remember
      the endless fags
         of times
      waiting, waiting, waiting
strung you
      with beads of sweat

I know
   you always remember
      the terrible taste
         of the one cigarette
            too many
          at three o'clock
            in the morning

but
   don't forget
   that long blue blow
      of the first drag

when everything
   is at last
      sweet.

I V

What's missing
    from this Melbourne moment
of cold hands
      sipping coffee
        over the newspaper?

A warm sigh
      of smoke.

V

My chilblained fingers
   fiddle
in the remembered warmth
   of an afternoon
      with Judy
         strolling through
            the briny languor
               of Paradise Beach

until
   shocked
      by a pink rip
         through a rock pool
we saw
   an octopus

its flash
   and fury
left us
   with splashed-out
      cigarettes

glamour-struck.

VI

My heart
   is visibly shivering

under my thin shirt

this afternoon is growing
   greyer and greyer

like your face

we don't talk for long

we smoke only one cigarette
each

after you go
I still smell
   like an ashtray.

VII

Why
   in the dust motes
      sparkling with the unreliable sun
         of this winter morning
am I conjuring
   the spirit of
      Alexander de Terres de Mottas?

Companion to Columbus
   scribbler, self-concealed
      Jew
         and my ancestor,
he gnawed
   his inquisitive way
through the exotic tangle
   of Cuba
returning home
   with the treasure
      of tobacco

I see him
   noisy, gauche, funny
      typically my family
then he dims
   falling away
      to his own
         austere company
and sacred fumes
   from the New World
prowling around his pen

faintly
   I see him
      wrestling his jaguars
        in Hebrew.

VIII

No wonder a pack of Benson & Hedges
    can still make my heart lurch

that fluttering palpitation
    of your memory

your house on the hill
and the window seat
    looking over the sea
where we'd sit lapping
        around each other
        and smoking
            your fags

at eighteen
    I was such a sucker
        for a grey-eyed woman
            leaning on my heart
            to light
                my cigarette.

IX

There's
   a space
between the exposed breast
   and the burning, burning
      cigarette

it's a cool space
   but thick
      as the human breath

and for a moment
   it holds his hand

deliberating
   in mid smoky air

until he remembers
   his orders.

X

The loneliness, the
   loneliness

of watching other
   on television
burning their sparkler lives
   right down to the butt

your own careful hands
   have never smoked

lying heavy
   like an unwanted dog
     on your lap

and warn you
   tonight
you might live forever.

XI

While you smoked
    the last cigarette
       in the packet

six and a half minutes
       passed

six and a half minutes
    rich, slow
       and sprouting
          from the loam
            of a mind at peace

six and a half minutes
    out of the cold rain
and cars
    splashing the gutter
       across your cuffs

six and a half minutes
    where you bloomed
       exotically
          along your bare branches
          like a magnolia
in this ceaseless winter.

SUMMER 92

AS CUNNING AS SERPENTS

You can cradle
   this snake's head
      for only so long

don't pretend
   you can push it away

the night outside
   flicks
      with spice and hiss

you're not wise
you're not peaceful

your spine is ringing
don't answer it

you can stroke
   this snake's belly
      for only so long

don't forget
your fingers will tell

they'll smell
   of indelible snake

is that what you want
that old reptile reek?

Melbourne 5/12/92

MY AT-LAST LOVER

Your face sleeps
    illuminated
in the early morning
    warmth
        of my slack arm

you're my at-last sound asleep
        child
you're my cat
    with a dreaming paw
        flexing in my hand
you're my raw storm
        gorgeously spent

and what am I, darling?

Exhausted

and full of trapped bubbles
    like honeycomb.

Sydney 18/12/92

MUD-CRABS

Under the price for a kilo
under
   this spasming summer

under
   the evenly tanned girls

oh, under my own skin!

are the tied-up-with-string
   mud-crabs

alive, just

moving like things
   in slow motion
      in warm humid air

not underwater
not their own lovely mud

their stalk red eyes
   move
      slowly
   in and out
   in and out

like my eyes
   in the dark
      with her

when I'm tied up with string

　　and waiting

but I don't wait
　　like a mud-crab

exhausted

　　with uncomprehending terror.

Sydney 30/12/92

PERFUME AND DROWSE

What makes our hands smoke?

What makes our fingers tigers?

We'd know each other
    in cinders

We'd know each other
    in stalk and spring

We'd know each other
    underwater

absent or present

We'd know
We'd always know.

But for now
    perfume and drowse
    perfume and drowse

for unreal and fabulous hours

hoarding each other
    like fragrant narcotics.

Melbourne 14/1/93

LASHED TO THE MAST

'Fortunate he who's made the voyage of Odysseus.
Fortunate if on setting out he's felt the rigging of a love
strong in his body, spreading there like veins where
the blood throbs.'

George Seferis

And what if the voyage
    slumps
in the peace of air-conditioning?

The sirens
    sing as throatily as Dietrich
from the white roses
        blazing in the garden

and you can't go to them

it's a sunstroke day

stillness starts
    in your cooling toes
and climbs
    like an anaesthetic

you can't move

let your rigging
    go slack
    go slap on your decks

let your blood
   crystallise

you can't move

it doesn't matter

nothing's calling
no-one's coming.

Melbourne 16/1/93

DROUGHT SONNET

After Lorca's 'Sonnets of Dark Love'

The parched weave of my shirt
soaks up your hand,
clothes, toes and throat.
Why am I this thirsty?

Every night
I sniff over
the wilting stretch
of my own hot skin.

Your mouth falls
so generously
on my mouth of sand

my tongue follows
mirage after mirage
along the wet of your lips.

Melbourne 21/1/93

'STUPID AS A POET'

After Juan Davila

Vanilla.
       That
too sweet. sweet. sweet.
       ice-cream
              of Girls' Talk
                     Girls' Poems.

Girls' Skin.

Flayed.
       So slowly.

We'd taste each
              other

Different.

Would your blood
       taste like
a salt lake
       lapping the back of my throat

staining
       the grooves of my mouth
              forever?

My skin breaks open
     like bread
its yeasty smell
     rises
like a flock of gulping ghosts

do you want me
   for lunch?

Take me with wine.
Turn my water to blood.
Your Blood.

Girls are just
       snails
trailing their delicious slime
right along the ironed edge
   of your seeping self.

When do we wash
   each other

Unsticky?

Do we want to be so

Clean?

Contaminate me instead.

Bring this poem
to your mouth

and suck it
till I die.

Melbourne 26/1/93

As Cunning as Serpents

You can cradle
this snake's head
for only so long

don't pretend
you can push it away

the right outside
flicks
with spice and hiss

you're not wise
you're not peaceful

your spine is ringing
don't answer it

you can stroke
this snake's belly
for only so long

②

don't forget
your fingos will tell
they'll smell
of indelible snake
is that what you want?
that old reptile reek?

JP. 1/12/92
Copy Melbourne
Airport for
Andy

Written 6/12/92
Oakleigh

love
P XXOO

132

AWAKE

"Lay your sleeping head,
human, on my faithless arm"
          W. H. Auden

For Andy
much
love
Dotty
xxxx

Your face sleeps
      illuminated
in the early morning
      warmth
      of my slack arm

you're my at-last sound asleep
      child
you're my cat
      with a dreaming paw
         flexing in my hand
you're my raw storm
      gorgeously spent
and what am I, darling?
Exhausted
   and full of trapped bubbles
      like honeycomb.
            18/12/92

Perfune + Dowse
~~What makes us~~ (21/1/93)

for Andy

What makes our hands smoke?
What makes our fingers tigers?
We'd know each other
   in cinders
We'd know each other.
      in stalk and spring

We'd know each other
   underwater

absent or present

we'd know
we'd always know
the spark words ~~to sing~~.

(2)

But for now
  perfume and drowse
  perfume and drowse
for unreal and fabulous hours
hoarding each other
  like ^{flagrant} narcotics.
  ~~against the future~~.

P 14/1/93
much love
Dolly X

Toorah,
Melbourne.

(from Summer '92-93)

Drought Sonnet

The fucked weave of my shirt
soaks up your hand,
clothes, toes and throat.
Why am I so thirsty?

Every night
I sniff over
the wilting stretch
of my own hot skin.

Your mouth falls
so generously
on my mouth of sand

my tongue follows
mirage after mirage
along the wet of your lips.

for A
much love
D XXX

26/1/13
Hawksburn.

ACKNOWLEDGEMENTS

I would like to thank the Literature Board of the Australia Council for its considerable support, and the following publications and their editors: *Island, Southerly, Eureka Street, Picador New Writing 1 & 3, Meanjin, Weddings and Wives* (Penguin 1994), the *Sydney Morning Herald, four W, Hobo, Voices, Sligo.*

I would also like to acknowledge the novel, *Prince of the Lilies* by Rod Jones, the inspirational trigger for the 'Crete' poems. This book reeks of Minoan magic and led me to the awesome labyrinth of *The Palace of Minos at Knossos,* Arthur Evans's six volume account of his excavations on Crete from 1921 to 1935.

I am grateful to the following for permission to reproduce copyright material: Penguin Books UK for the extract from *Selected Poems* by Osip Mandelstam (1977), Perdita Schnaffer for the extract from 'The Flowering of the Rod' by H. D. (from *Collected Poems, 1912-1944,* New Directions, 1986), W. W. Norton for the extract from 'Twenty-one Love Poems' by Adrienne Rich (from *The Fact of a Doorframe,* Norton, 1981), Faber & Faber for the extract from George Steiner's *Real Presences* (1989), Jonathan Cape for the extract from 'Upon a Foreign Verse' by George Seferis (translated by Edmund Keeley and Philip Sherrard) from his *Collected Poems, 1924-1955* (1973), and Alfred A. Knopf for the extracts from *nightingale fever—Russian Poets in Revolution* by Ronald Hingley (1981).

ligature *un*tapped

This print edition published in collaboration with Brio Books,
an imprint of Booktopia Group Ltd

Level 6, 1A Homebush Bay Drive · Rhodes NSW 2138 · Australia

Print ISBN: 9781761281006

briobooks.com.au

brio BOOKS

FSC
www.fsc.org

MIX
Paper from
responsible sources
FSC® C008194

The paper in this book is FSC® certified.
FSC® promotes environmentally responsible,
socially beneficial and economically viable
management of the world's forests.